Love, Life, and Limitations

BY EVOYNE H. BRANCHE

DORRANCE
PUBLISHING CO
EST. 1920
PITTSBURGH, PENNSYLVANIA 15238

Dorrance Publishing Co
585 Alpha Drive
Suite 103
Pittsburgh, PA 15238
Visit our website at *www.dorrancebookstore.com*

ISBN: 979-8-88812-103-0
eISBN: 979-8-88812-603-5

Love, Life, and Limitations

Acknowledgements

This book is dedicated to my family and friends who have always encouraged and inspired me. To my childhood sweet heart and husband Russell, who so diligently put up with me through all of my madness and whims. Thank you for the inspiration you have given me down through the years. To my childhood friends whom I hold near and dear for all of the conversations and heartfelt stories we have shared down through the years. To the men and women who serve in the United States Military for all of your encouragement and bravery and for letting me be a friend to so many of you. To my friend Kim who has inspired and encouraged me by reading what I write and pushing me forward. I will forever be grateful to you my dear friend. To the men and women of the FAA Southern Region, you inspired me so much thank you for your patience, hard work and diligence. I cannot tell you the place you hold in my heart and how much inspiration you have given me. To the Dorrance Publishing Staff and team members, thank you for helping me achieve a milestone in my life. I thank all of you for what you have done to make this book of love, life and limitations a dream come true.

I Am a Poet

I am a poet
Can't you see
There is so much deep inside of me
My dreams, my hopes, my faith to share
My stories of children and thoughts to compare

I am a poet… yes indeed
I need to tell you of what I see
I need to tell of thought unfurled
Of treasure to be found around the world

Of sea and pirate
Of bird and beast
Of great battles and medieval feast

Of worldly woes
and corrupted foes
Of love and kindnesses and good deeds done
Of Children laughing and having fun

Of shining stars that hold the magic
Of wonderful things and even the tragic
I am a poet… unknown I may be
But deep down inside there is a poet in me

A Dog's Love My Best Friend

When I am sad she holds me
When I cry she wipes my tears away
When my heart is broken right by my side she stays
When I fall she catches me
And helps me up with glee
When I am feeling lonely she does the funniest things
So much joy and happiness this friend brings

When I am happy she laughs out loud with me
When I want to dance she dances along with glee
When I am thinking she stares contently at me
Waiting for the time when I will be free

When I play my instruments she sings along with me
And she sings so loud the neighbors turn around to see
When I go walking she walks along with me
Stopping and greeting everyone she sees

Yes I love her wholeheartedly
Because she's the gal that truly loves me
No matter what condition I am in
She is my one and only true without a doubt friend
With me she is loving and Kind and never crappy
And yes my Doggie is the Girl that makes me very happy.

A Friend

When you have a friend who checks on you
A person who won't try to manipulate you or tell you what to do

A person who has your best interest at heart
A person who does not pretend and knows who you really are

A person you can depend on when things get tough
A person who knows how to tell you Hey that's enough

A person that will tell you when you are right or wrong
A person whose patience with you is very long

A person who wants nothing but the best for you
A person who treats you like you are valuable

A person who cares for you and does not have ulterior motives
A person who is always there for you and is devoted

A person who runs to you when you need a helping hand
And is always helping you work your plan

A person who cheers and roots for you
A person who chose to be a great friend to you

Keep that person close in your lifetime
Because trust me those kinds of friends are hard to find.

Vacant Space

When you're around you leave me breathless
And staring into space
I am not trying to be careless
Just trying to hide my face
Trying not to show you
How much I really care
Trying not to smile
As if you were not there
Trying not to leave a trace
Of what I feel for you
Trying not to leave a vacant space
Or reveal the truth
It's hard to imagine you and I together
It's hard to imagine knowing the truth
That we were never meant to be
I am just pulling the tree up by the root
Trying to hide the smile on my face
Of what I feel for you
Trying not to leave a vacant space
That would reveal the truth
When you come near me
I can hardly stand the beating of my heart
When you look into my eyes
The pounding of my heart starts
When you stand too close to me
Or we are face to face
My whole world melts around me
You leave no vacant space

Vacant spaces are not good
For those who fall in love
Vacant spaces only hide
The meaning of true love

Let's leave no vacant spaces
Let's hold each other tight
Let's cuddle and snuggle together
 All through the night

Let's leave no vacant spaces
We know just what we share
Our love for each other
And how much we care

For tomorrow is not a promise
That we can surely keep
So let's just love each other awake or asleep
For time is not always on our side
Let's leave no vacant spaces
Let's not hide

Let's love each other through thick and the thin
Through even the good and bad times
And even when we're hurting
Let's not leave a space behind

For vacant spaces separate us
And keep us apart
But let's continue to love each other
With all of our heart.

Be Yourself

Be yourself, be the best you that you can be
For there is only one of you and you need to be free

You have been given a once in a lifetime gift
The gift was given freely and to boost your spirit and give you a lift

No one can do what you do exactly the same way that you do it.
That is why being you is so very important

God gave it to you.
It's yours and cannot be duplicated.
He gave it to you even though you did not deserve it

Love yourself from the inside out.
If you do this you will learn what you are all about

You will glow from the inside and you will attract
Love, respect, admiration, and those who have your back
Those who will appreciate your energy and your gift
Everything starts with you and how you feel about yourself from within
God thinks you are worthy so start feeling that way
You are valuable and deserving of recciving thc bcst of lifc's pay

Be magnetic, loving, honest, and sincere and you will find
That there is no other you for truly you are one of a kind.

Boxed Intentions

Intentions are the things we often plan to do
The kind of things we hope to see all the way through
But sometimes things don't always go as we have planned
And our intentions are boxed up and never land

Intentions to loving without detours and limits
The kind of love that last a lifetime and not just for minutes

Intentions to having the kind of hope that reaches way up high
The kind of intentional hope that reaches for the sky
The kind of hope that makes it so easy to tell
 Of our intentions to wish everyone well

Intentions of forever faith that will never give up
Unboxed happiness, love, joy, and hope
Intentional faith that will never ever die
And lets you stand tall and hold your head up high

Intentions to help those who are in critical need
Unboxed intentions to help and lead
Helping to lead the world to be a better place
And doing it all with unboxed intentional grace.

Boxed intentions keep us from doing our very best
It keeps our hands and hearts tied up and we do less
So unbox your intentions just let them loose
Do all the good things that you choose to do.

Busting Loose

You say you love me
But I know you don't
You want to change me
But my answer is no
I like me just the way I am
I am not changing who I am for no man
It's time to focus on me and not you
From all the big fights, long nights
That you put me through
You think I need you
But we are through
This is the new me
I am busting loose

You claim you don't know what to do
You left me crying and heartbroken
That's what you put me through
You think I need you
But we are through
This is the new me
I am busting loose

Free from a love that never existed
Free from a love that was so one sided and twisted
Free from a love that could not be seen
Free from a love that is callous and mean
You think I need you
But we are through
This is the new me
I am busting loose

Free from a heart that was as cold as ice
Free from a hardcore love with a vice
Free from a love that is awfully grim
Free from a devastated heart within
You think I need you
But we are through
This is the new me
I am busting loose

Confusion

Sometimes without knowing it we cause confusion
Whether it's of the mind or just a delusion
Doing the kind of things that stir up trouble
Hey, I am stating a fact and not trying to burst your bubble

Sometimes we cast an illusion
That's the start of a daunting confusion
It causes others to see what we are not
And we wonder why our friends depart

Sometimes without thinking it through, we cause a panic
It causes delirium and things get manic
It causes confusion of our mental state
And then we don't know how to get it off our plate

Sometimes our relationships become a terrible mess
And we lose out even though we try our best
But what we see is our own conclusion
Of what was done out of a state of confusion

Sometimes we are baffled by things we see and do
It's often hard to understand and to interpret the view
That we are human and we are real
Despite of what we might ultimately feel

Confusion is the result of bewilderment
And of all the things we cannot interpret yet
But nevertheless let this one fact be true
Don't let Confusion be a part of you

Ever Sunny Blues

When I met you I knew I loved you
Don't ask me how, Baby I just knew
Then you went away
Now I sing the blues
Although I see the sky is clear
Dreaming of you is what I choose
And wishing you were near
This is my ever sunny blues
Staring at the awesome moonlight
I can feel you that's the truth
Because you are not here
This is my ever sunny blues
I just want to see
That warm smile on your face
I just want to love on you
In our special place
Although I see the sky is clear
I wish that you were here
I am always thinking of you
This is my ever sunny blues
Walking around looking at the ground
As if I did not have a clue
But this is the endless trend
Of my ever sunny Blues
The world is full of beauty
With bright colorful hues
But I cannot sleep without you
This is my ever sunny blues
Baby come back I need you so
Baby come back I didn't want you to go
You're the only one I choose
Who can take away my ever sunny blues

Fall In Love

Fall in love with someone who will take care of your heart
Who will keep you safe and out of the way of harm

Someone who will give you their heart
and bare their soul to you
Someone who trusts you to tell their secrets to

Someone who makes you happy and who makes you laugh
Someone who smiles at you whenever you cross their path

Someone who no matter how hard things get will never ever cheat
Someone who cherishes you from the first time you meet

Someone who will send you a good morning text
That says today I wish you the very best

That says I woke up with you on my mind
Someone who knows this treasure of love
Is so hard to find
Someone who does this every day
Someone who is content with you and wants to stay

Fall in love with someone who really wants you and waits for you
Who respects, cherishes, and admonishes you

Who understands when you are going through your madness
Who doesn't mind comforting you when you are going through some sadness

Fall in love with someone who helps and guides you
And knows all the things you are going through

Someone who will support you and root for your hopes
Someone who's on your side when things look hopeless and lost

Someone who talks and laughs with you after you have a fight
Someone who is helplessly in love with you and thinks of you all night

Someone who can be your peace when you have a problem
Someone who sits with you all night and tries to help you solve them

When love is real and love is true it will find its way
To your waiting heart each and every day

Love is pure of heart, mind, body, and soul
It is that something in you that makes you take hold
Of the fact that when you fall in love you are not you
And all things around you look amazing and brand new

Loving someone should be your biggest glory
So love them with all your heart
Let them be the end of your story

Forbidden Love

A forbidden love is a love you should not have
It can be humiliating and nevertheless it's sad
That two people cannot be in love
Others might become discriminatory and mad
That you have a kind of love they have never had

Love that is pure, sacred, and sentimental
Love that is honest, innocent, and gentle
Don't let it be tampered with by those who live in fear
Because even though it's forbidden your love is sincere

Don't let doubts cloud your mind
Or you might leave your love behind
And regret it for the rest of your life
Living with guilt and unsurmountable strife

Just let it flow like the ocean under a pale moonlight
Let your love be the light in the sky
Let your love be oh so sweet
When once your true love you meet.

Don't hide it in a cold dark closet
Let it soar and soar like a rocket
Live, love, and be happy
And enjoy your love life freely

Heart and Soul

When you dig down deep inside yourself
You might see that you need help
To let yourself be loving and kind
And not leave anyone or anything lovable behind
Dig down deep and you will see what life is all about
Compassion, forgiveness, mercy, and concern
These things are in your heart without a doubt
Do you love without favor?
Do you care about your neighbor?
Do you love the things you do?
To thine own self be true
Do you forgive and forget
Or do you still hold on to the things you regret
Can you love without a cause?
Or do you see others flaws
Do you laugh at yourself?
Or do you make fun of someone else
Do you lend a helping hand?
And help others out as much as you can
Does your heart coincide with your soul?
To see your character, thinking, and perception unfold
Do you reason with kindness or do you reason with contempt
Do you have memories of your time well spent?
Reasoning and feeling the right things to do
Is your conscious reality and it's a part of you
When your heart and soul coincide
You will feel their presence deep down inside
And everything will look beautiful and in place
That's your heart and soul leaving its trace.
It's a beautiful thing to see
Letting your heart and soul run free
And clearing your mind of all doubt
And loving yourself from the inside out.

Hot Hot Hot

I hear you talking
And you're hot hot hot
I see you walking
And you're hot to trot
I see your smile and it hits the spot
When you dance boy you Rock Rock Rock

I hear you humming and it's top top tops
And when you sing it is off the charts
When you play your tunes you just show the world
That you are magnificent at what you hurl

So do your thing and let the world see
Just what an amazing man you can be
It's awesome to see your name in lights
And to hear your name screamed from great heights

So when I see you I just smile smile smile
You're on top of the World and I love your style
So keep on doing the things you do
And I will keep cheering and rooting for you

In Another Lifetime

In another lifetime I think we met
And I imagine the time we spent
Laughing, fighting, and having fun
And those kinds of memories cannot be undone

In another lifetime, I swear I knew you
I don't know where, how or when
But every so often, I feel you, feel you,
feel you, deep down within

Tick Toc how the time flies
Tick Toc no time for goodbyes
Tick Toc one thing is true
My love of a lifetime is always you

In another universe maybe you were there
It's really hard to know just when or where
It's not in a face, a smile or your eyes
But it's the person on the inside I will recognize
In another space and time you left the faintest trace
As the wind blew I felt you touch my face
If in a dream we should ever meet again
I hope I still have these memories of you my timeless
Love and friend

Tick Toc how the time flies
Tick Toc no time for goodbyes
Tick Toc I am missing you
My love of a lifetime is always you

If you should ever walk into my space
Even if I don't recognize your face
I would know by the fluttering of my heart

I would know that you were an exciting part
Of a memory I won't forget
And therefore I would have no regrets

Something beautiful has taken place
In another time and another space
You were beside me all this time
And this forever love is only mine

Tick Toc how time flies
Tick Toc no time for goodbyes
Tick Toc one thing is true
My love of a lifetime is always you

Even if it were for just a little while
I felt your presence and you made me smile
And when I feel you, you calm all my fears
And when you leave I just shed tears

Tick Toc how time flies
Tick Toc no time for goodbyes
Tick Toc I am missing you
My love of a lifetime is always you

Just Let Me Love You

There are times when I see you standing there
Looking sad and in pain
I think about what I could do to help you smile
And make you love again
Just let me love you
And make you feel alive again
Just let me love you
You have nothing to lose and a lot to gain

You stand there expressionless
And my mind says to just let you be
But my heart says to love you
And let you fly away and be free
Just let me love you
And make you feel alive again
Just let me love you
You have nothing to lose and a lot to gain

Let me wrap my arms around you
Let me whisper in your ear
Let me hold you oh so tightly
Let me keep you close and near
Just let me love you
And make you feel alive again
Just let me love you
You have nothing to lose and a lot to gain

Time will soon pass us by
And soon you will see
That you will always have a friend
In me

Lasting Impressions

In my life I have been blessed
To travel around the world to the Orient and more
I met such wonderful people
Who opened their hearts and doors
People who comforted and nourished me
People who gave me hope
People who wiped my tears away
And laughed at my awful jokes
People who took me shopping
When I did not have a car
People who just loved me
From near and afar
People whose smiling faces
Just really made my day
People who took the time
To show me kindness along the way
People that I will never forget
Who taught me valuable lessons
Those family and friends
Who left great Lasting Impressions
Impressions on my heart
Impressions on my mind
Impressions that will last an entire lifetime
Impressions on my spirit
That inspired and left me motivated
Impressions in my soul
That were uplifting and elevating
For that I am so grateful and thankful indeed
For you left your
Lasting Impressions forever with me

Just Plain Ole Me

I often sit and wonder how this world would be
If I were someone else and not just plain ole me
Plain ole me likes having fun
Laughing and being silly
But then again that's just plain ole me

Plain ole me likes looking at the stars
And gazing at moonlight
And walking in the rain, making a snowman
And watching TV at night

And I often take a walk and wonder how it would be
If I were someplace else that did not allow me to be me

See the me in me likes lots of things
That makes the world's beauty
Like rainbows and flowers
And that big ole apple tree

I like how the Pyramids seem to peek toward the sky
And how the statue of Liberty holds her lamp up high
Have you ever seen the Oceans Waves?
And the beauty of the fish in the Sea
I like that kind of beauty but then that's plain ole me

 Plain ole me is helpful, dependable, loyal, and kind
Plain ole me is a tough independent chick
And I refuse to complain and whine
Plain ole me loves dancing
 And doing the silly things
That only being happy and having joy can bring

So when someone yells out, "Hey! Who the hell is she?"
I turn around, smile and say, "It's just plain ole me"
The reason why I am happy and how I stay free
Is because I allow the me in me to be just plain ole me
And yes, sometimes people don't like what they see
But I will just continue to be just plain ole me

Plain ole me likes sitting around in her underwear
With those pink foam curlers wrapped around in her hair
And plain ole me likes window shopping
Yeah sometimes I am stone cold broke
And sometimes plain ole me likes playing a practical joke
And just in case you're wondering how it would be
To be plain ole you like I am being plain ole me
Just take away the fancy stuff
And just be yourself
Take your pride and selfishness
 And store it someplace else

Let your mind and spirit dance and be fancy free
Then you will enjoy the happiness of being you
Like I enjoy being plain ole me

Leave all your issues, trauma, and drama behind your skeleton door
Because life has a lot to offer, to life there is so much more
Once you've done that just sit back, relax, and be free
And enjoy your life of being you… like I enjoy being plain ole me.

Just The Way I Am

I love spending time with you
But sometimes I like to be alone
It gives me time to think of you
My heart's not made of stone
I need someone who really likes me
Who loves me just the same
Someone who really knows me
And loves me just the way I am
I can be a bit carefree
I can be a bit aloof
But the one thing I know for sure
Is that I love earnestly and that's the truth
I need someone who really sees me
Who loves me just the same
Someone who really knows me
And loves me just the way I am
I know there are things that are not meant to be
There is so much to you and a lot more to me
There are differences in life that we can't hide
And then there is always the question of our pride

I am not trying to hide anything or the way I feel
I am just saying out loud let's be for real
The truth is and I'm just making it plain
I just need to be loved just the way I am.
Love me just the way I am
Love the real me
Love me just the way I am
Let's see how great love can be

Lessons Learned

Finding out who you are
May seem petty and hard
But you need to know
What makes you tick and how you roll

Lessons learned can be just what you need
So that your heart, mind, and soul can be free

Lessons learned will help you grow
Your spirit in Love will actually glow
Lessons learned teach us what to do
To make it through life and show the best of you

Lessons learned teach us how to cope
With life's hard knocks and harmful pokes

Lessons learned show us the way
To cope with hate, doubt, and fear every day

Lessons learned is a mighty tool
That teaches us how not be a fool
It teaches us to learn the facts
Before we say or do anything rash

It teaches us how to react
To adversity and discrimination
And how to take back
Our lives with determination

Lessons learned teach us in retrospect
What went well, what went wrong, and what answers were the best

It teaches us how to be safe and handle critical situations
Our lessons learned have no limitations
On life, liberty, and our pursuit of happiness
And help us achieve our true awareness
Of who we are and where we should be
In life, in love and reality

So learn your lessons well my friend
So you can finally be happy in the end
And achieve all your goals
It's your duty to know how your life unfolds

Life Without Regret

There is wonderment in living this gifted life
Oh yes God gave it to us and he did not think twice
He gave you gifts and undeserved talent
And he winked his eye at you when you finally found it
The gift of love is the greatest of all
To love life without regret is a wonderful call
To humanity and all that is within
He gave you the gift of being forgiving
He gave you the gift of words to speak
And of morals and of values to teach
He gave the gift of poetry to make us think
For the words we write are penned in ink
So they can be kept forever and a day
In books, online, and in our hearts as we read them always
The gift of languages which could be called tongues
Is used to tell all the good things that can be done
For God has blessed us one and all
Each of us has a heavenly call
Then he gave us a gift of prophesy
So that we can live our lives more responsibly
Rooted in God's word and divine revelations
It is the Holy Spirits way of communicating
And is given and received by the people of the Godhead
So that their spirits would be heavenly fed
This gift is absolutely binding and holds the truth
Of the great love God has for you

So live your life without regret
For the Love of God is not finished with us yet

Life's Imitations

Living your life can be full of mind-blowing activities
But be sure to know your limitations
Everything in life is not cut and dry
if you are not paying attention some things might pass you by
What is a limitation, you might ask?
A limitation is a barrier or a restriction on a thought or task
It can hinder you from doing things you want to achieve
It can put a stop on the things you request or might receive
It is the thing that prevents you from being at your maximum potential
It can cause strife in your life and slow down things you think are essential
Such as dealing with others on a daily basis
Or slowing down an idea and not being hasty
It can slow down how you perceive love
And cause you to hide your mind in a cove
It is the thing that deters your decision making
Causes fear, heartache, and lack of determination
Language barriers can play a part too
But somehow in life we make new friends and manage to make it though
It is a roadblock of mind-altering and heartbreaking causes that you will regret
 Because you placed undeserved limitations on it
So find a way to get around your limitations
And your mind-altering sensations
Find a way to be determined in your quests and be marvelous in your actions
So that you are magnificently proficient and have passion
About your life and what you want to do
Let it be the brand new you
And let your plan work its way to its rightful destination
And don't let your mind and things in life become limitations

Pillow Talk

When we lay our heads on our pillows
And talk to each other
We talk about deep things that happen
Beneath and above the covers
We talk about feelings left unsaid
The kind that can only be said in bed
We talk about things that hurt and pierce our hearts
We talk about things that we wanted to say and do
But never got to start
We talk about the old and the new
We talk about how our love grew
We talk about the future and the past
We talk about the things that did not last
We talk about things that make us happy
We talk about the things we take for granted
We talk about our highs and our lows
We talk about our dos and our don'ts
We talk about how to make our lives and love more stable
We talk about putting our wants on the table
We talk about our wildest dreams
We talk about taking feelings for each other to the extreme
We talk about the truth that will set us free
We talk about what's deep down inside of you and me
One thing is for sure when we have pillow talk and nothing is blocked
Because the one thing we know is that our loving one another will never stop

Loving someone should never be a secret
Because not being able to reveal it is just like sleeping
Sleeping I might dream of you
But when I wake up I know it's not true

Secret love is worse than that
You know it's real but you have to turn your back
And pretend that your secret love is not there
And lie about it as if you don't care

When all the time they have your heart
And you want them to be known and not depart
If the one you love has to be a secret
Then you might as well not have a love just let it go and not keep it

But down deep in your heart you know that you love
And cherish your sweet little secret
But you don't want the world to know or you might lose it
And not be able to keep it

So you hide your secret in a very dark place
So others cannot see your face
Or see you smile when they are near
And hear your heart skipping beats in fear

That you are in love with someone they might not agree
Is the right person for you
But nevertheless your secret love is the best thing that ever happened to you

So let the world know about your secret love
And don't hide it anymore
Your secret love may open up so many other doors
And make you happier than you can imagine
Because this kind of love might hold magic

Magic that you cannot possibly understand
That the love of your life can be your best friend
This kind of love proves Love can exist without reasons and boundaries
And give you a lifetime of wonderful and endearing memories

The Business of the Mind

Our mind is the thing responsible for all mental phenomena
That keeps us focused on the things going on around us
Like thought, memories, mental images, will, and sensation
Also perception, pain, belief, desire, emotions, and intention.

The business of the mind is very unique
It keeps us on our toes so that we are at our peak
Of understanding what is really going on
The good, the bad, the ugly, and also the wrong

The mind is a masterpiece of invention
That's keeps us focused and steers us in the right direction
It's up to us to make it work with supreme responsibility
That helps us keep our lives and our bodies up to extreme mobility

From the rising of the sun to the wonderful moonlight
The mind is constantly at work giving us insight
Of things to love, cherish, and hold in high esteem
To keep our hearts, souls, and our bodies clean

The mind helps to keep us going in all the right directions
And inadvertently steers us to make necessary corrections
In the methods we use to communicate with others without hesitation
And to make new friends without reservation

When we don't let the mind do its awesome job
Then we make mistakes and we are robbed
Of all the good things we have learned
And all the wonderful moments we could earn

Of our hopes and dreams that help to inspire
Of the real things we desire
Of the things we think are unobtainable
Oh yes the mind makes us awesomely trainable

So the mind is the one thing that keeps us focused
The mind is humanities exceptional bonus

It gives us courage to make it through hard times
And helps us through our lives to unwind

And to challenge ourselves on a daily basis
To face our fears through every crisis

It is said that a mind is a terrible thing to waste
And that is right because your mind can never be replaced.
So don't load it with lots of foolishness
Give it a break and let it rest
So it can operate at its peak
So that your mind is never weak

Unconditional

There are lots of things in life that come with a condition
Like illness, addictions, and marital afflictions
Like eating something that doesn't agree with you
And getting dizzy when you did not want to
Like wanting to be part of a group who ridicules you
All of these are conditions of a people who missed the unconditional clue

Unconditional means you do it without looking for fortune or fame
You give it without seeking gratitude or emotional strain
You say it from the depths of your heart
You do it often and on time like the ticking of a clock
You portray it without giving it another thought
With a smile on your face you gave it with love

You say it and mean it with love in your voice
And the twinkle in your eyes show that it was an unconditional choice
You give hugs when they are needed and cry too sometimes
Because that's the beauty of your unconditional side

When hurting you feel it but you soon let it go
Without wanting an apology or wanting to gloat
It's unlimited, undeserved, and wholehearted the giving
Of one's heart among those of the living

Unconditional means you love without wanting something in return
It means you give your love even if it's undeserved
It means that God has given you a heart that is made of Gold
It would take a really hot fire to melt the hold
Of the loving unconditional side of you
May your life be full of gratitude
For you have loved with faith and have shown
The love of God in its truest form.

When Love Dies

When we first met and fell in love
We started out as friends
You held me close and gently
Whispering you loved me in my ear

You looked deep into my eyes
And told me how you felt
Kissed my lips while holding my face
Causing my heart to melt

What happens when love dies
Or fades over time
No more kissing, hugging
And making love
No more rhythm to our rhymes

My heart aches and I feel faint
When thinking of where love went
I feel disappointed and hurt
But I loved you without regret

I am sorry that it did not last
As we move on to someone new
But this is what happens when love dies
It will break your heart in two

When Two Hearts Collide

Some people may not think this is true
But I want you to know I thoroughly thought it through
Your world can be whatever you love and admire
It can be the one thing that takes you higher

Some people's worlds are what's in their hearts
The person they love is a great place to start
So when two worlds in heart and love collide
It's a feeling that will never ever die

Their worlds collide into one another causing a big bang
It explodes and causes the hearts to boomerang
But instead of breaking up and falling apart
The collision causes love to build up

Their love builds and grows and blossoms with surprise
It grows and gets fertilized before their very eyes
This love grows and cannot be contaminated
Because nature covers it and it is laminated

Because it is a love that was predetermined in nature
It gives the hearts a great deal of pleasure
When two hearts collide and fall into the right place
It's hard to pry them apart and it can never be replaced

This collision of love is like a grand firecracker
That keeps the hearts together like it's guarded by a linebacker
It's hot, it's colorful and it sparkles with pride
It glows and flows like the ocean's tides

It culminates into the most musical sounds
The hearts beating pound after pound

It makes the ground tremble and opens wide
The heart to feel something so strong inside

Like the love of another you can feel when you're apart
But the waves of the heart and its love is like creating a fine piece of art

A collision of fate, time, and persona
Is like witnessing the flares of a supernova
You ask what kind of love is this
It's the kind that has been touched by God's own hand and it's sealed
with a kiss
Guarded carefully through time and space
Their hearts and their love are eternally interlaced

With an Open Heart

I don't know what you did
But oh you sure did it right
You got a hold on me
And now you have my heart
I don't know what to do
I don't know how to act
All I feel is you
In every beat of my heart

My heart is wide open
Come get me my love
My heart is wide open
Babe I'm ready to give it up

I don't care how you want it
I just want you to know
My heart is wide open
And my love is ready to flow
I don't know what to say
I don't know what to do
All I know is that right now
 My heart is open to you

My heart is wide open
Come and get my love
My heart is wide open
Babe I'm ready to give it up

My love is flowing and it's really hot
All I need is you and you know how to hit the spot
If you want me like I want you come and get this love
Baby you are all I can think of

My heart is wide open
 All I want is you
My heart is wide open
Show me what to do
My heart is wide open Babe it's you, you, you

The Girls

Who would think that there would be a myth
About what a girl's gift is
Is she a good girl let's see
What in the world should a good girl be
Should she be kind hearted, generous, and graceful
A practical woman who is supremely tasteful
Should her dress be classy and above board
Should she be educated, well-groomed and one who is adored?
Is she one who is loved by many?
What kind of man should her man be?
Talking about the bad girl is something to think about
Is she like one of the boys just lurking about?
Is she loud, crass, crude, and rude?
Is she a fighter and not one to brood?
Does she show you her true heart?
Or does she hide her feelings in the dark
Is she loud and extremely boisterous?
And thinks out loud with a cussing voice
Does she dress for the world to see?
Her breast, her hips, her legs, and anything in between
Sometimes she is educated and sometimes she is not
But for the man who loves this type of woman
She steals his heart
Well here is how I see it with my own two eyes
In every woman the good girl and the bad girl resides
It depends on who her man is
If he's a good boy who likes the bad girl who dresses less
Or a bad boy who likes the good girl who has a lot of finesse
Or is he a man who knows how to dig deep inside
To unleash the girl who she tries to hide
Beneath the skin that she lives in
And lets her be herself with him
Because in each girl there is good and bad

She can be made happy or she can be made sad
And when the right man steps up
He will be happy to see
The kind of woman he needs her to be
And when this happens true love blooms
And good girl and bad girl feelings zoom
Higher and higher than can ever be known
Until she finds the man that will call her his own
And when that's done
There is nothing left but fun, fun, fun.

Cause and Effect of Being In Love

Being in love is beautiful and very natural but it can be scary as well
For we know not the reason of love or what it tells
There are things that cause us to fall in love
And make us feel different then we felt before

We feel as if butterflies are in our stomachs
And we have awkwardly odd moments
Sometimes we feel just plain silly
And sometimes we shiver like it's a bit chilly

It gives us a feeling of being highly intoxicated without ever having a drink
It makes us feel childish and giggly and we cannot think
It's the action of being fulfilled from the inside out
And wanting to say I love you out loud

The effects of love are not always clear
Except how much you love that boy or girl
The feeling makes you feel like being on top of a mountain
And like you have drunk from a holy fountain

It's a feeling that makes you feel little shocks of electricity all through
your body
Make being around or seeing that person your top priority
Although love has causes and effects plus ups and downs
It's still like well sown seeds in the ground

And hope the one you love is always near
And showing them how much you care
When we see the person we start to feel strange
And all of a sudden we want to change

Because we know not what to do
The effects leave us feeling nervous and mischievous too

Doing things that lovingly say I love you
While our hearts thumping loud and rapidly too

There is a sudden rush of emotions such as happiness
And the feeling that you cannot catch your breath
It will make you feel more beautiful or handsome
While feeling like you will never again be lonesome

Being near them makes you feel secure
And your giving them your love seems innocent and pure

And even though love is sometimes not perfect
It is one of the things in life that gives us purpose
So love with all that you have to give
Do it faithfully, be brave, and just live.

It may make you think that everything else in the world does not matter
For love is the part of life that makes you feel better

Loves Phenomena

Love is emotion coupled with intimacy, passion, and commitment
And it needs trust, care, affection, attraction, closeness, and attention
It works its magic in our hearts by unusual or remarkable occurrences
That leads us to the one whose love is our convergence

Loves Phenomenon is very unexplainable
And sure to make us feel like it's unobtainable
Its true essence is tempered with the unspeakable gift of the joy we get
When once our true love is met

We sparkle, we shine, we glisten, and we glow
Like the beauty of the awesomeness of fresh falling snow
The melody in our hearts is loud and clear
Whenever the love of our life appears
It's the way they walk and glide into view
Or they speak and their words hang onto your heart like glue

Loves Phenomena says you are the sun in my life, the wind that brushes
across my face and every beat of my heart
It says you put the smile on my face and you did it from the start
It says that when you hold hands they melt together like a hand in a glove
And while holding hands you can actually feel the love

It says I want to love you and hold you so tight that all the broken pieces
of your life melt back together
And that come what may, I want to be with you in any kind of weather
It says you are my dream that has come to life
And I will love you with all my might
It says I want to be your joy and your peace
All day, all night, awake, or asleep

It says words can never express how much I love you but my heart speaks
it every day
And it is my unconditional plan to love you always
It says even though you have made mistakes and may have weaknesses
I still find you truly amazing
And I love you and give my love to you without hesitating

For love and affection is greater than perfection
And it deserves all of our attention